Build positive character traits one letter
at a time with

ABCs for Me!

A workbook for the young learner

Part of the Young Parenting Series

ABCs for Me!

A workbook for the young learner

Part of the Young Parenting Series

Created and written by
Juliann G. Mangino, Ed.D.

Clip art and/or font copyright Dianne J. Hook, www.djinkers.com. License No. 189246908.

ISBN-13: 978-0-9967370-2-9

Ordering Information:

Special discounts are available on quantity purchases. For details, contact the publisher at docpublishing@yahoo.com.

Doc Publishing

Dedication

One Sunday morning my husband, Matt, our twins, Mark and Melina, and myself, went out for breakfast at a restaurant about 40 miles from our home. We enjoyed the usual conversation and discussion about what each of us would order for our meal.

As we finished placing our order a large table of children and adults had just finished their meal. As the mother of three of the children was gathering her things we caught each other's eyes. We both smiled and simultaneously asked how each other has been. You see, this young mother, Jenna*, was one of my students in the teen parenting program for which I serve as counselor.

Jenna pointed her three young boys out to me and was quick to point out the two oldest, now 9 and 7, were the two children she had as a teen mother. She caught the boys' attention and announced, "Boys, you see this lady here…she helped me quite a bit when you were very small. She made sure I graduated high school." This comment warmed my heart.

The boys walked up to my table and said "hello." One had a deck of cards and asked me to pick a card, any card. I did, and while he closed his eyes he asked me to place it back in the deck. I placed the card right on top in an attempt to make his trick a bit easier. He opened his eyes, took the card from the deck and announced, "Did you have the nine of hearts?" "I did! I did!" I said with shock and surprise at his magical powers. He waited a few seconds, leaned in towards my ear and said, "Ya know…I don't always get that right."

Now as Jenna was finalizing things she called out to her boys, "Let me see your face…let me see your face," and finally, "let me see your face." She made sure that all three of her boys had a clean face and clean hands before they left. As the boys left, I said to them, "Be good for your mother." They called back to me, "You be good too."

This is to whom I dedicate my book. To the many young parents I have had the pleasure of working with but, more importantly, I dedicate this book to the many children raised by those young parents.

*name has been replaced for privacy purposes

Table of Contents

Introduction

The Young Parenting Series includes *ABCs for Mommy!* and *ABCs for Daddy!*, both of which highlight positive character traits, or attributes, that promote positive parenting. These two books were written with parents and caregivers in mind. *ABCs for Me!* is written especially for the young learner, ages 4 to 7, to learn positive character traits during their most formative years.

According to the U. S. Department of Education, ninety percent of the brain's capacity is developed by the time a child reaches the age of five. Many early childhood programs align curricula, assessments and professional development to assure the continuity of early learning.

Much of the curriculum designed to promote early learning are aligned with state standards in the areas of Cognition, Language, Literacy, Perceptual, Motor, Social, Emotional, Science and Mathematics.

A variety of curriculum extends to the primary grades with the same goal alignment to state standards.

ABCs for Me! promotes the building of the whole person through early introduction to core attributes. The positive character traits, or attributes, also align with many areas of early learning standards and primary school standards.

The CASEL (Collaborative for Social and Emotional Learning) organization defines Social and Emotional Learning (SEL) as, "…the process which children, and adults, acquire and effectively apply the knowledge, attitudes, and skills necessary to understand and manage emotions, set and achieve positive goals, feel and show empathy for others, establish and maintain positive relationships, and make responsible decisions."

There are five core competencies of SEL that can be taught in a variety of ways and in a variety of settings. *ABCs for Me!*

is one of those tools for teaching Social and Emotional Learning, covering all five core competencies:

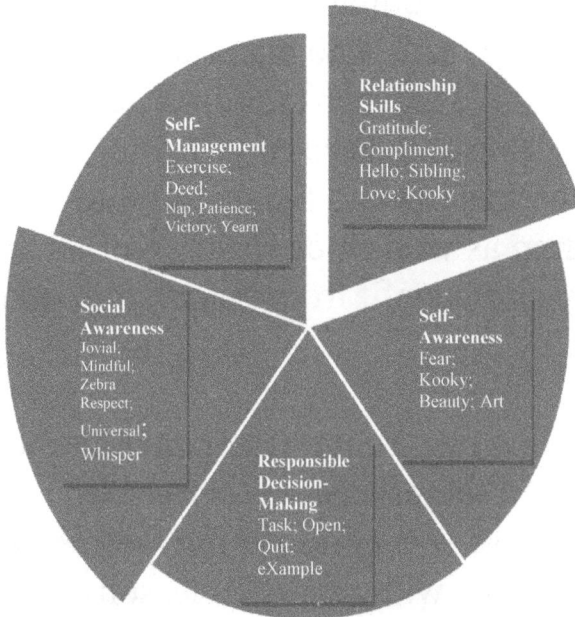

Relationship Skills
Gratitude;
Compliment;
Hello; Sibling;
Love; Kooky

Self-Management
Exercise;
Deed;
Nap, Patience;
Victory; Yearn

Social Awareness
Jovial;
Mindful;
Zebra
Respect;
Universal;
Whisper

Self-Awareness
Fear;
Kooky;
Beauty; Art

Responsible Decision-Making
Task; Open;
Quit;
eXample

*The above chart lists the positive character traits from **ABCs for Me!** and how each connect to Social and Emotional Learning (SEL).*

- Self-Awareness;
- Self-Management;
- Social Awareness;
- Relationship Skills; and
- Responsible Decision-Making.

This workbook is designed for Pre-K through grade 2. For the Pre-K through Grade 1 the book is meant to be used with the teacher/facilitator or parent/caretaker taking the lead. The material is read to the child with a teacher/facilitator leading instruction and discussion. The author encourages reading the material to the older children as well since children of all ages enjoy and benefit from listening to others read.

In a classroom of younger learners, there is a larger-size *ABCs for Me! Interactive strategies for the new learner, Pre-K to K*, with modified lessons, available. Allowing space for small hands to write big, the modified workbook may be provided for each student while the teacher/facilitator conducts the reading portion of the lesson from the book.

The teacher/facilitator can opt to utilize *ABCs for Me!* in 35 short, easy and fun lessons for children. With one lesson per week for 9 months the workbook can be utilized the entire school year.

The intent of this year-long unit is for the teacher/facilitator to read the lesson to the children allowing time for the student to listen, follow the reading, reflect, learn and interact with the lessons that follow each of the positive character traits.

Once the lesson is delivered for the week the positive character trait should be posted in the room for ongoing reinforcement.

Additionally, there are positive character trait reviews that follow a cluster of three introduced positive character traits. During the reviews the students have the opportunity to use shapes, colors, trace and write as they connect to social and emotional learning.

ABCs for Me! sparks conversation too! Because of the interesting positive character traits, or attributes, that are introduced, many children will enjoy sharing their opinion.

ABCs for Me! also includes Poet's Corner. Poet's Corner is comprised of four poems that are found throughout the book. The poems have been chosen with the young heart and soul in mind.

Soon the young learners will appreciate poems as a form of literature that is both speech and song—with a whole lot of meaning.

Whether you are using this workbook as a parent, caregiver, teacher or counselor, it is my hope that you will find the positive character traits to be ones that are worth promoting.

How Many, How Much
by Shel Silverstein

How many slams in an old screen door?
    Depends how loud you shut it.

How many slices in a bread?
    Depends how thin you cut it.

How much good inside a day?
    Depends how good you live 'em.

How much love inside a friend?
    Depends how much you give 'em.

ABCs for Me!

A is for **Art**—
    A way to express your feelings.

B is for **Beauty**—
    See it in others, inside and out.

C is for **Compliment**—
    Give one every day.

D is for **Deed**—
    Always let it be a good one.

E is for **Exercise**—
    60 minutes every day.

F is for **Fear**—
    Overcome and try new things.

G is for **Gratitude**—
    For what you have.

H is for **Hello**—
    Both a gesture and a greeting.

I is for **Interests**—
> Search for yours.

J is for **Jovial**—
> Don't worry, be happy.

K is for **Kooky**—
> Make someone laugh today.

L is for **Love**—
> Your family and one another.

M is for **Mindful**—
> Be where your feet are.

N is for **Nap**—
> Take one and feel refreshed.

O is for **Open**—
> Your mind to see the world around
> you.

P is for **Patience**—
> Slow down, take your time.

Q is for **Quit**—
> NEVER do this.

R is for **Respect**—
>Show this in action and words.

S is for **Sibling**—
>A brother or sister.

T is for **Task**—
>Do one and save-a-step.

U is for **Universal**—
>Learn this language.

V is for **Victory**—
>When you reach your goals.

W is for **Whisper**—
>The softest of your soft voice.

X is for **eXample**—
>Set a good one.

Y is for **Yearn**——
>To learn more & more (& more).

Z is for **Zebra**—
>What color are your stripes?

A

is for **Art—**
a way to express
your feelings.

Whether you draw, color, paint, use clay or Silly Putty you are making something that expresses your feelings. This is your art.

It can be very helpful for you to use art as a way to show others how you feel. You can choose to draw how you are feeling instead of trying to find the right words to explain your feelings.

Think of how many ways you can use art. You can draw your feelings and thoughts, you can paint your dreams, or you can color what you want to be when you grow up.

Art is something that everyone can do, whether you are a child or adult, young or young at heart.

A is for Art

<u>Art Lesson</u>

Using crayons, colored pencils or markers, draw how you feel today.

Do you feel happy, tired, mad or excited?

Whatever you are feeling, draw it on the next page.

How Do You Feel Today?

B is for **Beauty**—
see it in others, inside
and out.

What do you think of beauty? Beauty is not only how things look to us but is also how we feel about ourselves and what is around us.

We should all try to notice the beauty in ourselves. Do you like being a good helper? Do you like to sing or dance? It is important to notice the beauty in yourself and be proud.

It is also important to recognize the beauty in your friends, family and neighbors. There is beauty in everyone, sometimes we just need to take the time to find it.

Once we see the beauty in things and people around us we begin to live life in a happier way.

B is for Beauty

Beauty Lesson

Circle whether you think the statement is True or False.

True or False

Beauty is only the way someone looks.

True or False

There is beauty in everyone.

True or False

If we see beauty, we can be happier.

C is for **Compliment**— give one every day.

A compliment is when you share praise that makes someone feel good about themselves.

If someone says to you "I like the way you help others," they are giving you a compliment and that makes you feel good.

It would be great for all of us to give compliments to each other. When you practice giving compliments, and do it often, it will be easier for you to notice when people deserve a compliment. It will also make it easier for others to compliment you—and for you to accept those compliments, and feel good about yourself.

You could start at home. Compliment

your mom, dad, grandmother, grandfather, brother, sister or anyone else in your home. Take the time to think about your compliment.

An easy compliment is to notice what people do well. Something like, "Mom, I like the way you pack my lunch," that's a great compliment and will make mom feel good, and you feel good too!

C is for Compliment

Compliment Lesson

In this Compliment Lesson you are to write, draw or say a compliment to two people that are either related to or close to you.

Then do it again tomorrow—compliment them again or choose two new people to compliment.

3-Step Review—A, B, C

A is for Art—a way to express your
feelings.

B is for Beauty—see it in others, inside
and out.

C is for Compliment—give one every
day.

Let's go over what we learned so
far. A is for **Art** and you can use art as
a way to express yourself or to show
others what you are feeling or thinking.

B is for **Beauty**. Beauty is found
in everyone. We don't always need to
see beauty, it can be on the inside.
Search for everyone's beauty.

C is for **Compliment**. Every day
you should find a way to give a
compliment to others. You can

compliment with words or gestures, such as saying "I love you" or giving a hug.

Step 1

<u>Trace</u> the letters A, B, C using your finger and <u>say</u> the letter aloud.

Step 2

Color the letter "A" **blue,**

Color the letter "B" **green,**

Color the letter "C" **purple**.

Step 3

Draw a circle.

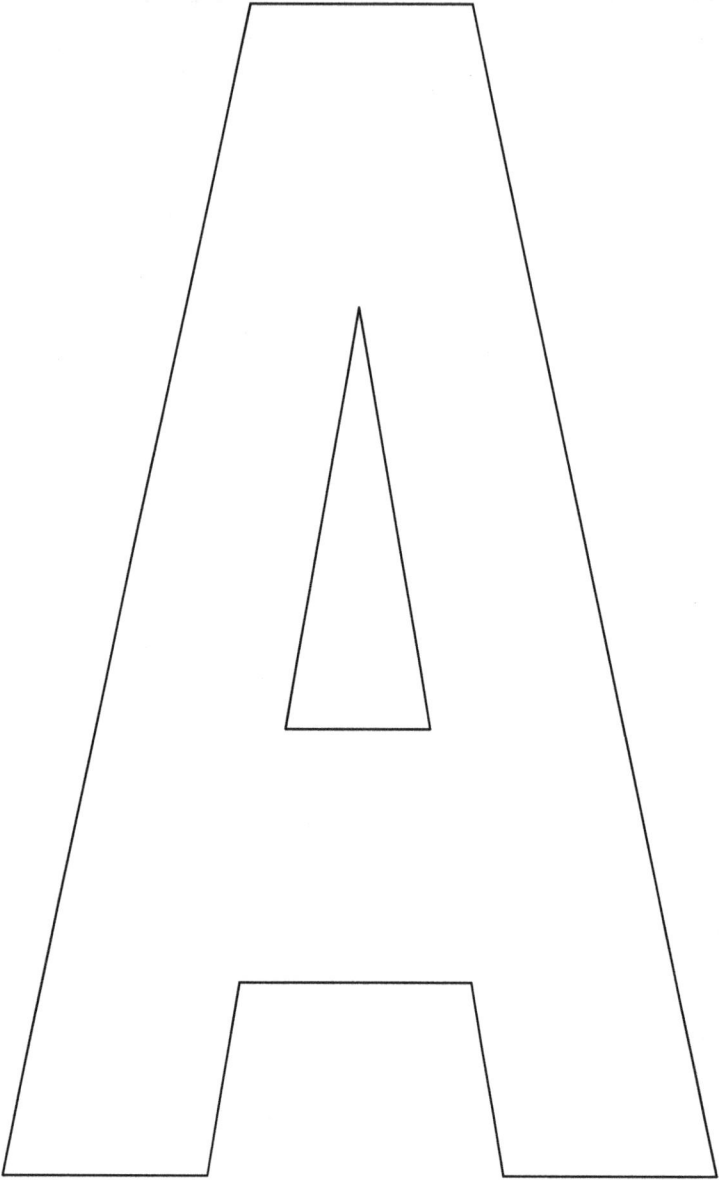

22

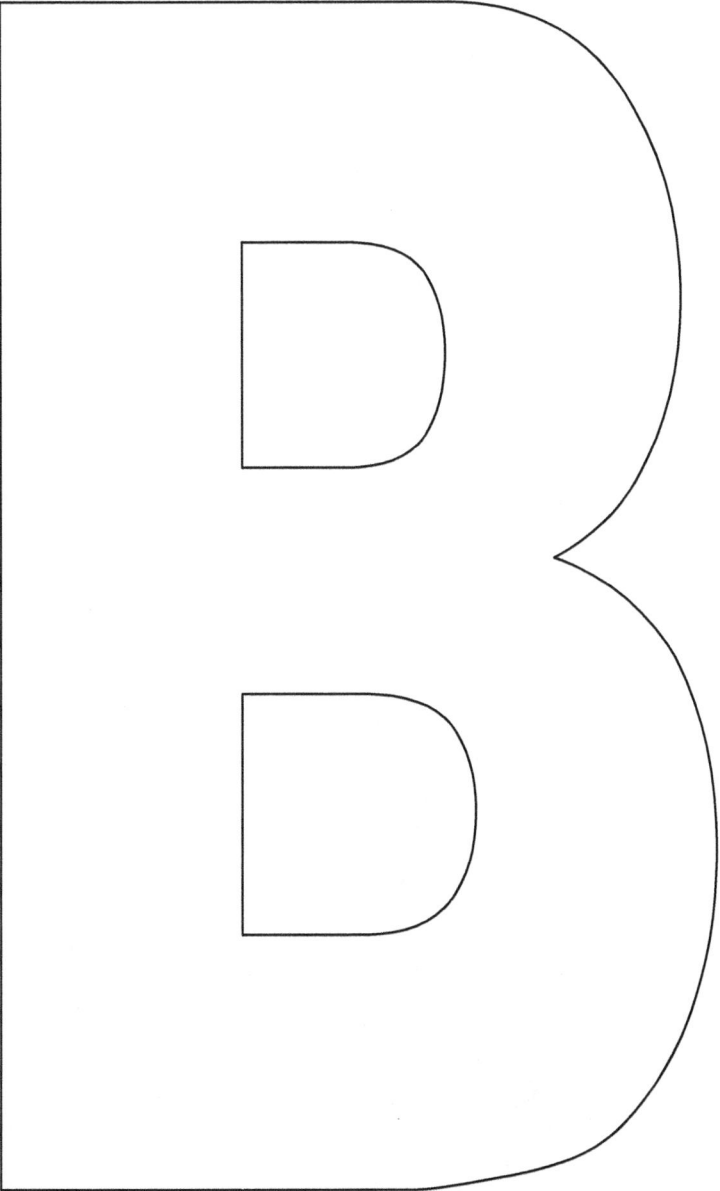

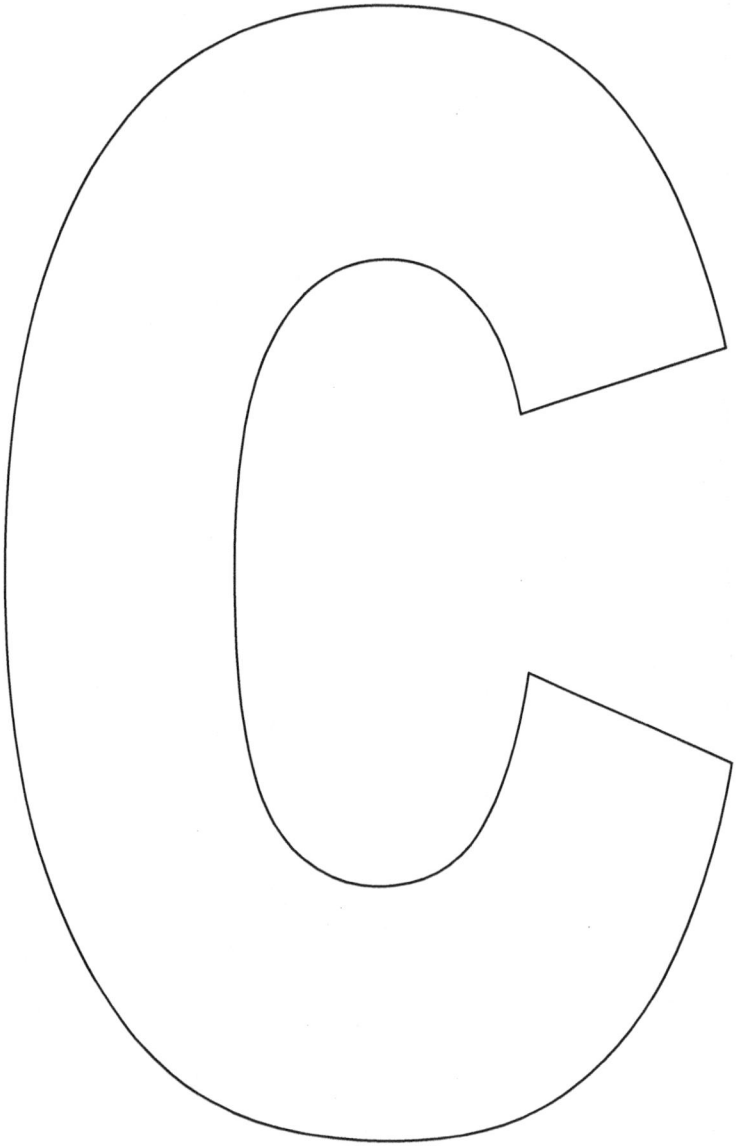

D is for **Deed**— always let it be a good one.

A deed is something that is done. A good deed is when you do something good for someone.

Let's say you are playing at your friend's house and his little brother is sad because no one is playing with him. If you and your friend include him, and play with him, that is doing a good deed.

When you do a good deed for someone, they may feel so good that they do a good deed for someone else. So your one good deed can turn into many more good deeds, which means many more happy people.

D is for Deed

Deed Lesson

It can be easy to do good deeds. All you have to do is help, support or appreciate someone.

For the Deed Lesson, let's think of ways we can do good deeds and talk about it. Then write or draw the good deed on the next page and explain.

What good deed can you do for this young boy?

Draw or write your good deed here.

E

is for **Exercise**—
60 minutes every day.

Exercise is fun, isn't it? Is it fun to jump, move your arms, play yard games, bicycle, skate, jump rope, play hopscotch, skip, or just run around? That kind of movement is exercise!

Exercise is not only fun—it is healthy. Yes, exercise and movement is good for you, and the more you do it—60 minutes every day—the healthier it is.

So why is exercise healthy for us? Exercise and movement helps us to stay at a healthy weight, it keeps our heart strong and helps us sleep better at night.

The National Football League (NFL) teamed up with the American Heart

Association to teach kids that 60 minutes of play every day is healthy and fun.

The NFL and the American Heart Association believe exercise helps us to work in teams, cooperate, be responsible and, most importantly, it keeps us healthy.

E is for Exercise

Exercise Lesson

If you, or someone in your family, has a smartphone or tablet, I challenge you to:

- Download the app, *NFL Play60*

- Use the app every day to help get your 60 minutes of exercise.

If you, or someone in your family, does not have a smartphone or tablet, I challenge you to:

- Get a notebook and keep track of your daily exercises.

- On a new sheet of paper every day, list the ways you exercised for that day.

Open a Book
by Jane Baskwill

Open a book
And you will find
People and places of every kind;

Open a book
And you can be
Anything that you want to be;

Open a book
And you can share
Wondrous worlds you find in there;

Open a book
And I will too,

You read to me
And I'll read to you.

F is for **Fear**— overcome and try new things.

There are some moments when we feel afraid—we are experiencing the emotion of fear. When you fear something or are afraid, you are worried that you, or someone you love, might be alone or need help. Fear is important at times because it alerts us to dangers.

There are times when we could be strong and go after the fear. If you are afraid of thunderstorms then maybe you could work at being strong during the next thunderstorm and allow yourself to understand that there is nothing to be afraid of, the noise of thunder is really just nature doing its job.

In order to work through your fears, it is important to stay calm, be strong, and the feeling of fear will pass.

F is for Fear

Fear Lesson

Let's practice memorizing this quote by President Franklin D. Roosevelt to keep calm when you are afraid.

"The only thing you have to fear is fear itself."

~Franklin D. Roosevelt~

Repeat:
The only thing…
The only thing…
The only thing…

Then repeat:
The only thing you have…
The only thing you have…
The only thing you have…

Then repeat:
The only thing you have to fear…
The only thing you have to fear…
The only thing you have to fear…

Then repeat:
The only thing you have to fear is fear itself.
The only thing you have to fear is fear itself.
The only thing you have to fear is fear itself.

Now say it aloud and you have it memorized.

The only thing you have to fear is fear itself.

3-Step Review—D, E, F

D is for Deed—always let it be a good one.

E is for Exercise—60 minutes every day.

F is for Fear—overcome and try new things.

Let's go over the last three attributes we learned. D is for **Deed** and a deed is something that is completed. To do a good deed for someone is when you have been helpful in some way.

E is for **Exercise**. Exercise is more than play time or recess. It is a time for us to work on being healthy. When we exercise we are working to keep our heart, muscles and bones healthy.

F is for **Fear**. We don't want to be afraid. But, fear is healthy and can alert us to dangers. Remember, the only thing you have to fear is fear itself—so when you feel afraid, stay calm and you may find that fear simply slips away.

Step 1

<u>Trace</u> the letters D, E, F using your finger and <u>say</u> the letter aloud.

Step 2

Color the letter "D" **black,**

Color the letter "E" **brown,**

Color the letter "F" **gray**.

Step 3

Draw a square.

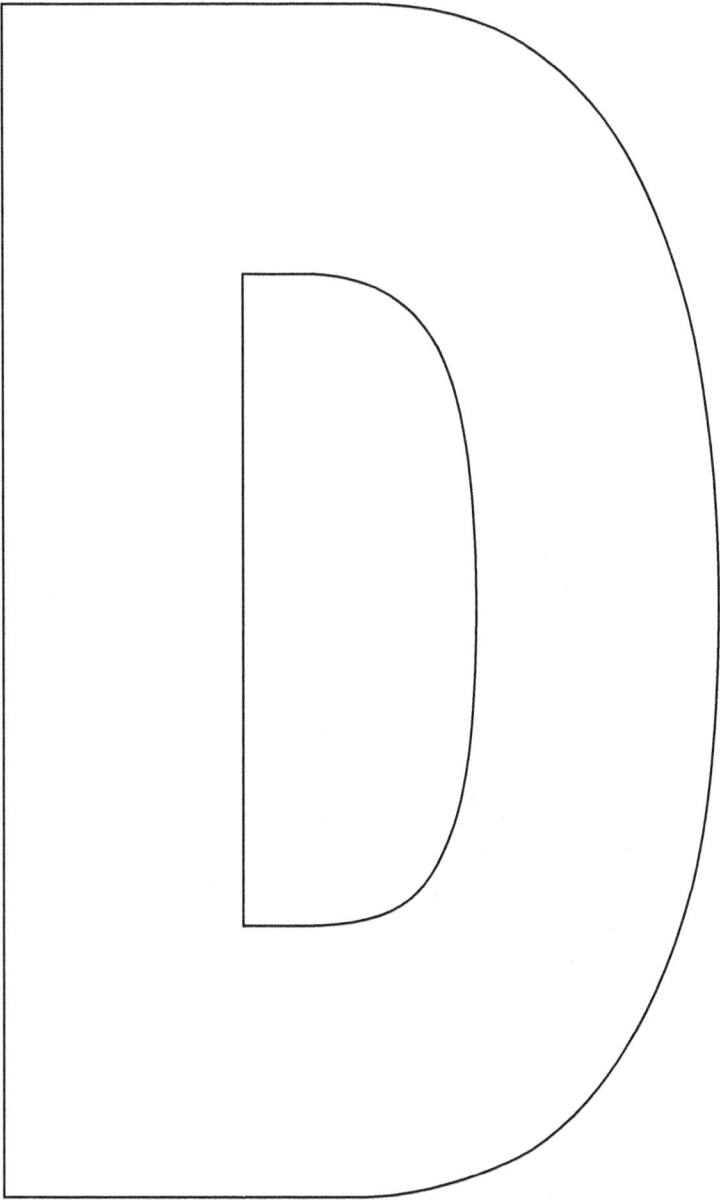

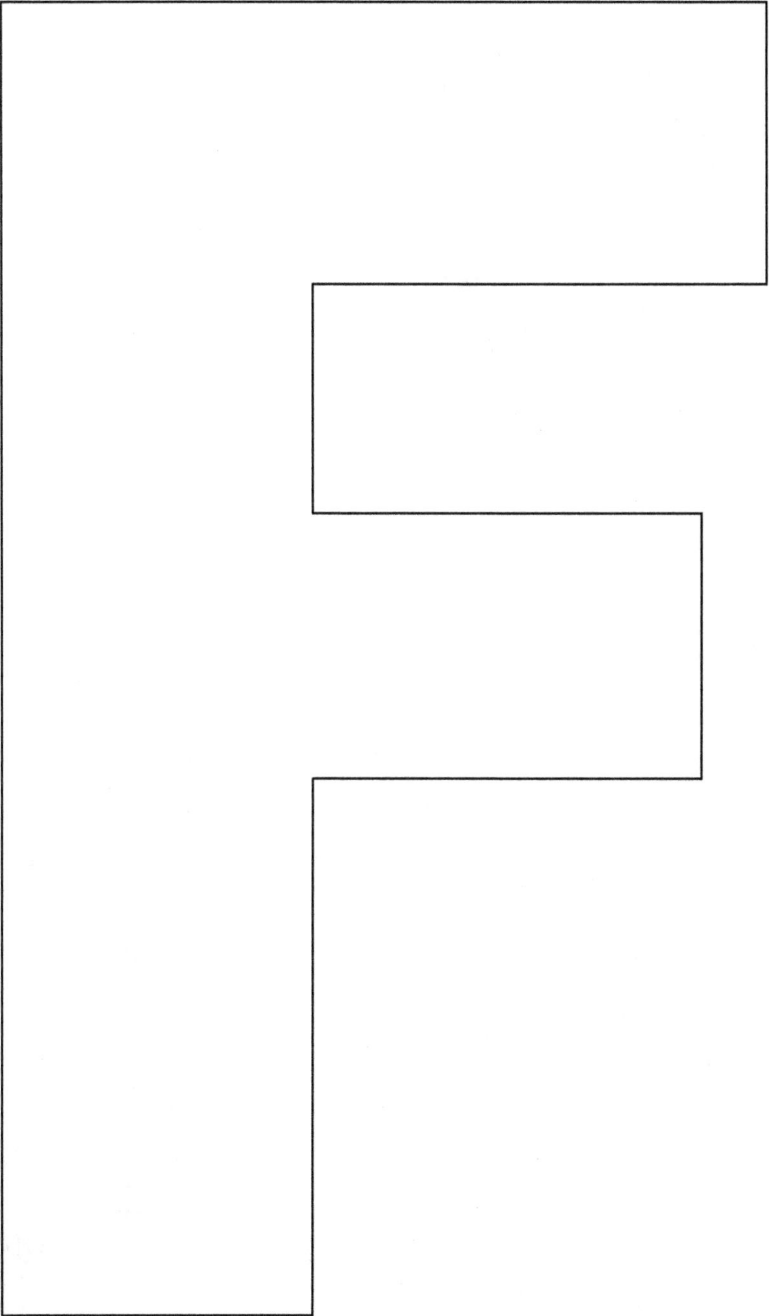

G is for **Gratitude**— for what you have.

Gratitude is a big word that means you give thanks for things that people do for you, get for you, or help you with.

Let's think of ways we could show our gratitude—show others how much you appreciate what they do for you. A simple hug shows others we care and is a way of saying you like them and thank them.

You can make a craft and give it to someone as a gift or as a gesture to show your gratitude.

Gratitude can also be expressed to someone just because you are glad they are a part of your life. Remember, gratitude doesn't cost a cent, but it's a gift that's worth a million bucks.

G is for Gratitude

Gratitude Lesson

Today you will write your first Gratitude Gram, or note, to say thanks.

Fill in the blanks by drawing pictures or choose words from the word box on the next page.

Dear _____ ,

Thank you for everything. Thank you for

_____ me and thank

you for _____ me.

Love,

_____
write your name here

Word choices

Mom   loving   helping   teacher

Dad   listening to   Grandma

reading to   Grandpa   playing with

H

is for **Hello**—
both a gesture and a
greeting.

To say "hello" is more than just a greeting. It is a word that should be said with a smile.

The smile you display when you say hello to a friend or stranger is showing that you care and that you are happy to see them.

When you say "hello" to someone you should do three things at the same time—smile, say "hello," and look the person in the eyes.

A "hello" greeting is used when you see a family member, a friend, a classmate or even someone you don't know, as a way to make a connection with that person.

An example might be when you are

taking a walk with someone in the park and someone walks by you, you might make eye contact and should say "hello" with a smile. You just might brighten their day.

It feels good to be noticed. When you say "hello", you are letting that person know that they are noticed.

H is for Hello

<u>Hello Lesson</u>

What are the 3 things you should do when you greet someone?

1. _____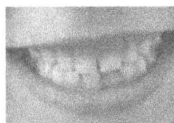

2. _____

3. _____

Challenge yourself to greet someone with "hello" today and every day.

I

is for **Interests**—
search for yours.

When you are interested in something you want to know more about it. When you are interested, you may often think about those things and are eager to learn more.

If you are interested in using Legos to build things you may want to play and build as much as you can. As you get older you may expand your interest into what it takes to build a building, bridge or boat.

For now, you may be interested in soccer, dance, gymnastics, t-ball or video games. Our interests change as we grow. Don't stop searching for what you love to do.

When you grow up you will be happiest if you are doing what you want to do and what you love to do.

I is for Interests

Interest Lesson

In this lesson you will learn about yourself.

Name_____

Student Interest Inventory

Read each question and circle the face that shows how you feel.

1. How do you feel about school?

2. Do you like to read?

3. Do you like to write?

4. How do you feel about math?

5. How do you feel about social studies?

6. How do you feel about science?

7. Do you enjoy music?

8. Do you enjoy art?

9. What are your strengths? _____

10. What would you like help with? _____

3-Step Review—G, H, I

G is for Gratitude—for what you have.

H is for Hello—both a gesture and a greeting.

I is for Interests—search for yours.

Let's go over the last three attributes we learned. G is for **Gratitude**. We should be grateful for what we have in life and we should let people know it.

H is for **Hello**. Hello can be used as a greeting or a simple gesture of friendship. Try to get comfortable looking people in the eyes, smiling and saying "hello."

I is for **Interests**. Always take an interest in how things are done around you. This will help you discover what interests you the most. Once you find what you are interested in, success will find you.

Step 1

<u>Trace</u> the letters G, H, I using your finger and <u>say</u> the letter name aloud.

Step 2

Color the letter "G" **red,**

Color the letter "H" **pink,**

Color the letter "I" **yellow**.

Step 3

Draw a triangle.

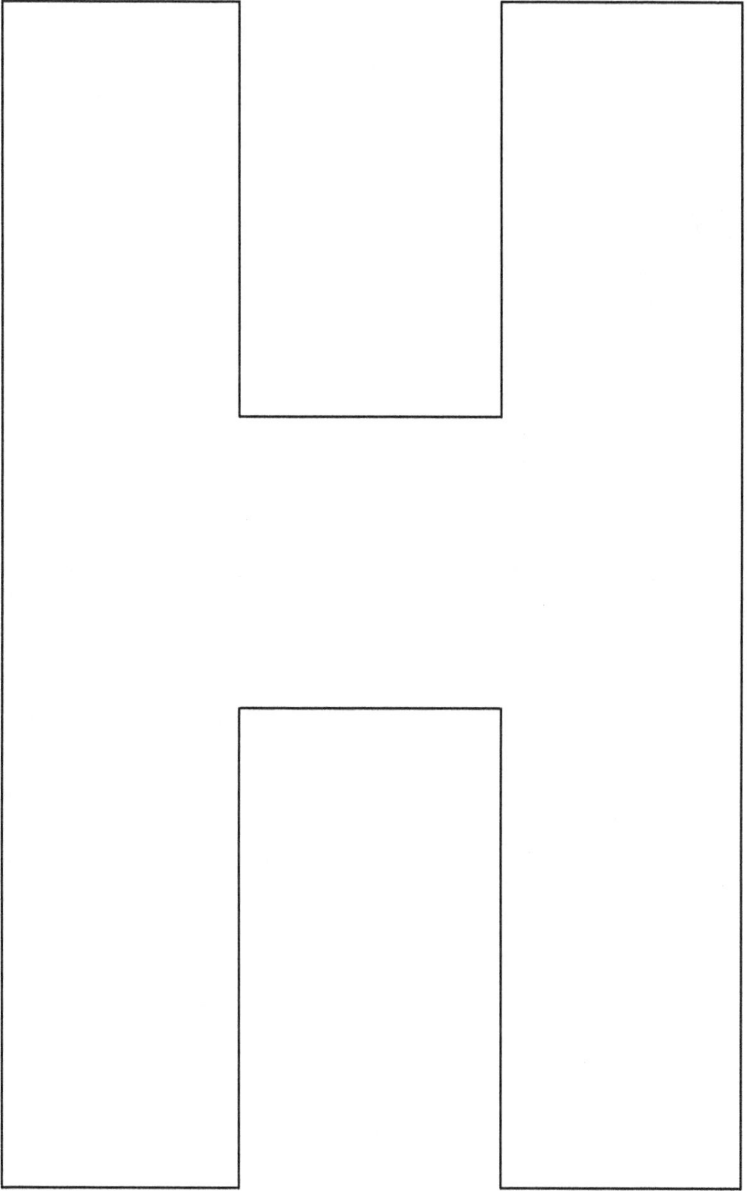

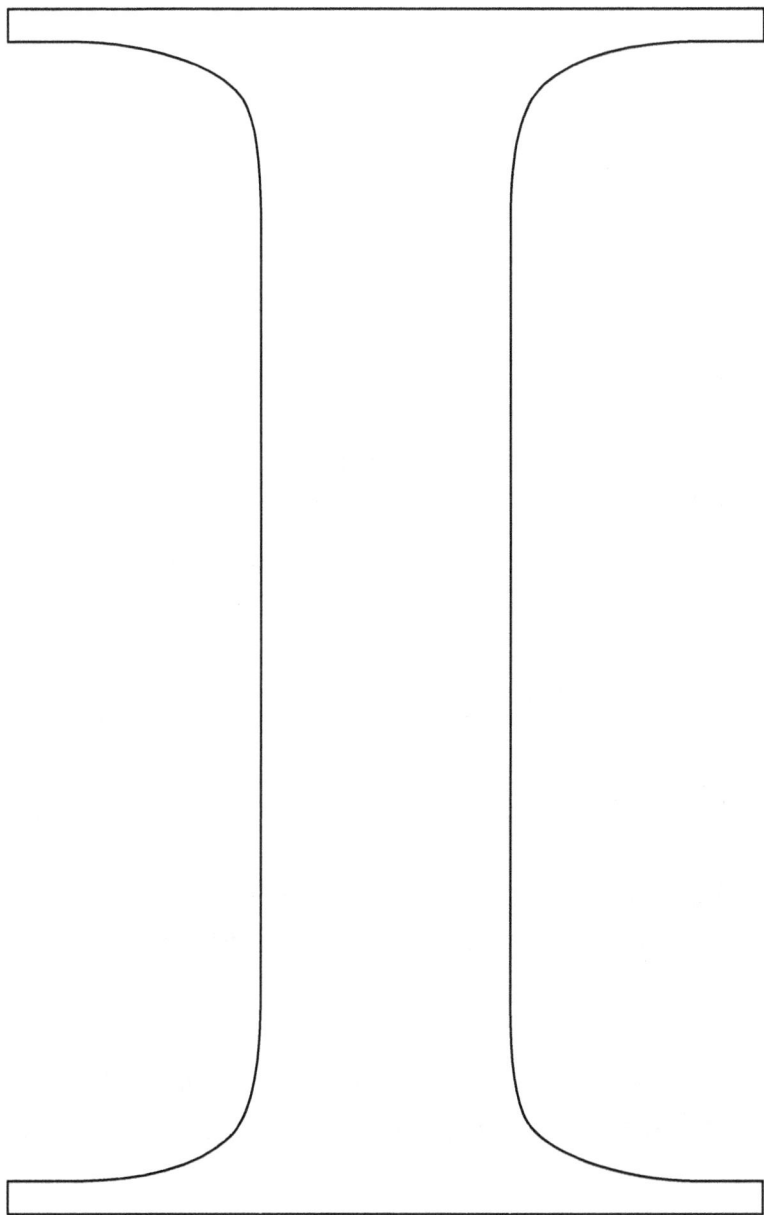

I

J

is for **Jovial**—
don't worry, be happy.

Don't worry, be happy. Bobby McFerrin put that simple phrase on the tip of everyone's tongue several years ago with his song, "Don't Worry, Be Happy." It is a fun song that tells us that we may all have troubles but if you worry it will only make your troubles seem bigger.

The song also goes on to tell us that when you are not happy, when you have a frown on your face, you will make others feel unhappy.

To be jovial means to be happy and look at the fun side of things.

Sometimes it is hard to be happy when things get tough. Remember it's not always

going to be tough and you have some
control over being happy.

Keep in mind the four words from that
song—don't worry, be happy.

J is for Jovial

Jovial Lesson

Practice smiling and turn your frown upside down – ☹ ☺.

Look in the mirror and see for yourself how a smile brightens your eyes and cheeks. A smile is catchy. It is hard not to smile at someone who is smiling at you.

Notice when you smile at someone that they will often smile right back at you, making everyone just a little happier.

K is for **Kooky**—make someone laugh today.

Can you make a funny face? Maybe cross your eyes and stick out your tongue? This is one way to be kooky.

When you are feeling relaxed and comfortable it is easy to be kooky and make friends and family laugh. You might want to tell a funny joke, do a funny dance, or take a few funny face selfies. Funny face selfies can be fun to look back on with your family and laugh again. When you laugh it seems as though the world is happy. Use your kookiness to make the world happy.

Do you know someone who you would describe as kooky or silly? If so, think about how he or she makes you laugh. What do they do that you enjoy the most?

K is for Kooky

Kooky Lesson

Tell these jokes to friends and family and see if you can make them laugh with your kookiness.

When a librarian goes fishing what does she use for bait?

Bookworms

What colors would you paint the sun and the wind?

The Sun rose and the Wind blue

What did the mother ghost say to the baby ghost when they got in the car?

Fasten your sheet belt

L

is for **Love**—
your family and one
another.

You grow up with the ones you love.
As babies, your parents or caregivers gave
you what you needed—food when you were
hungry, blankets when you were cold and
comfort when you were sick.

As you get older you will learn that
your parents or caregivers give things to you
not just because you need them but also
because they love you.

It is wonderful for you to give love
back to your family and to others. You can
show love in the way you talk, help others,
and in the way you thank others for the love
they show you.

Love is a special feeling you have for
another person. There are different kinds of

love. Love for a parent or caregiver may be different than the love for a sister, brother, or friend.

Love is also about respect. To have love and respect for someone means you admire them for who they are and value your relationship.

L is for Love

Love Lesson

Today, tell people you are close to that you love them. Complete this practice sentence. You may use the Phrase Bank to help you complete the sentence.

"Grandma, I love you because
_____."
fill in the blank

Phrase Bank

you take care of me

you play with me

you understand me

you make me laugh

Here is an example of what you might say…

"Grandma, I love you because <u>you</u>

<u>listen to me</u>."

3-Step Review—J, K, L

J is for Jovial—don't worry, be happy.

K is for Kooky—make someone laugh today.

L is for Love—your family and one another.

Let's go over the last three attributes we learned. J is for **Jovial**. Wake up happy and ready to have a great day.

K is for **Kooky**. When someone tells you that you are kooky take that as a compliment. When you are a bit kooky it means you don't take everything so serious and you enjoy life.

L is for **Love**. You love the people who are closest to you, and those who take care of you and keep you safe. But maybe you don't always tell them how much you love them. Tell those around you how much you love them.

Step 1

<u>Trace</u> the letters J, K, L using your finger and <u>say</u> the letter name aloud.

Step 2

Color the letter "J" **orange**,

Color the letter "K" **blue**,

Color the letter "L" **green**.

Step 3

Draw a rectangle.

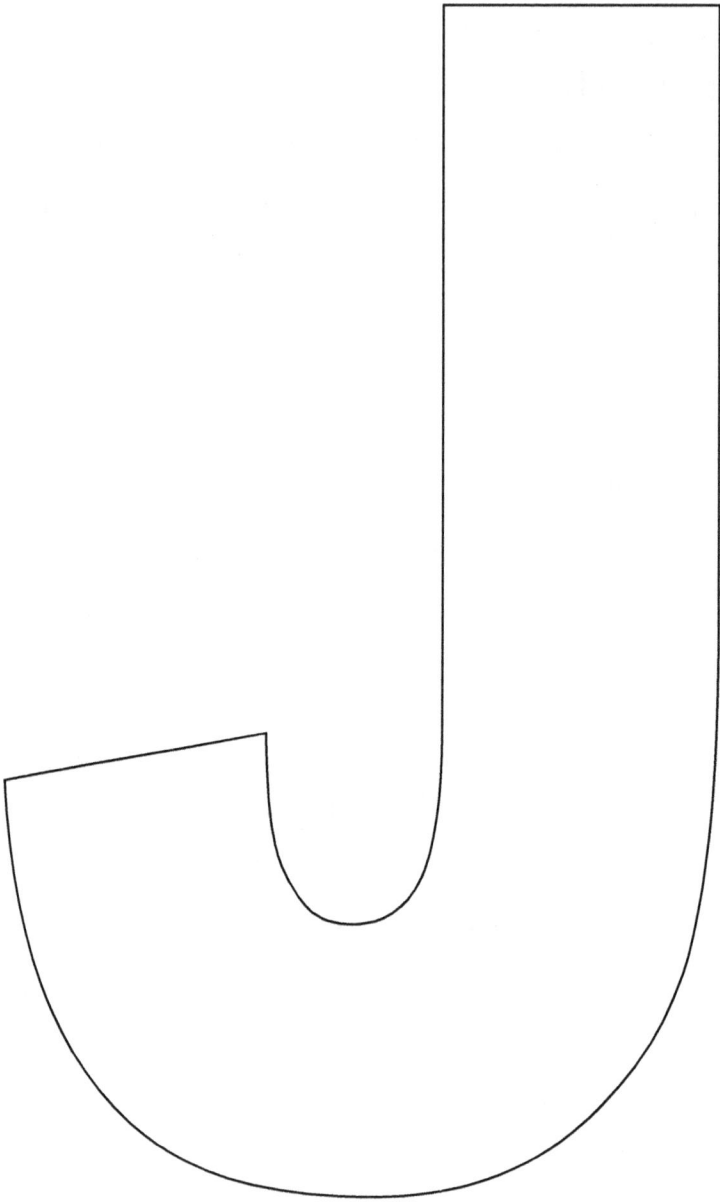

64

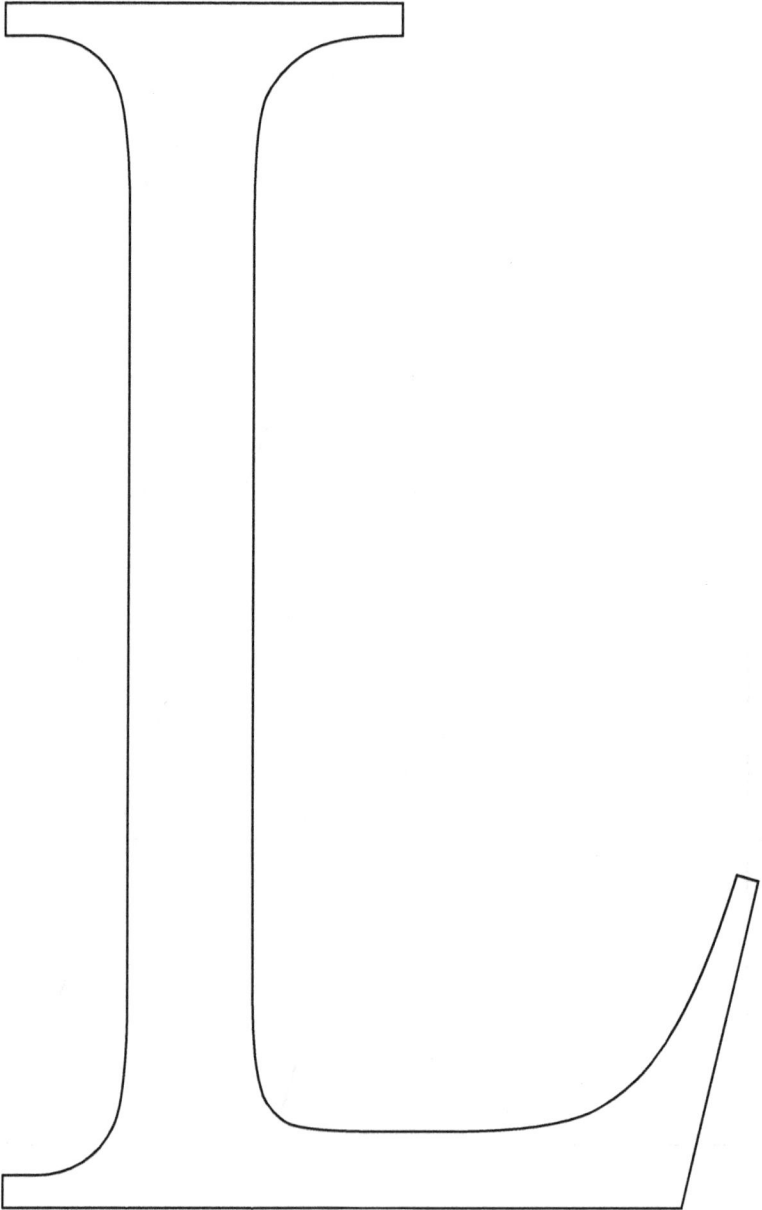

L

M is for **Mindful**— be where your feet are.

Every day we should take time to be mindful. To be mindful is to be in the moment, doing an activity without distraction. When you are where your feet are, you are giving full attention to whatever it is you are doing—everything else can wait.

As you begin this challenge to be mindful you may realize just how much you miss because you're not focused on the task at hand.

These days it seems a lot of our conversations with friends and family has at least one person with his head down while talking. We need to look each other in the eye while talking—you can't do that when you're looking at your iPhone. You can be a leader and remind family members to be where their feet are.

When eating at a restaurant with the family, notice how many people (adults and children) have their heads down looking at some sort of electronic device. Are they being mindful to where they are and who is around them?

We are missing a lot of living when we don't focus on where we are and what we are doing. Don't be distracted—focus on the task at hand.

M is for Mindful

<u>Mindful Lesson</u>

If we all do our part we can help spread the word to be where your feet are.

Today, tomorrow and whenever you think of it, when you see someone looking down at a handheld device and not paying attention to those around her you should suggest to that person to—

"Be where your feet are."

Just maybe they will begin to understand that we could all pay a little more attention to things around us.

N is for **Nap**—
take one and feel refreshed.

Do you remember taking naps? Maybe you still take naps during the day. Taking a nap can feel very good and give you more energy for the rest of the day.

Naps can be taken at any age. In some countries it is a custom to take a rest (or nap) every afternoon. In those countries stores sometimes close during this time so everyone can rest. Can you imagine mommy or daddy coming home to take a nap?!

Some school children think naps are for babies—but they aren't. Naps are for everyone of all ages to help their body get the rest it needs, have more energy to think and learn better.

You need to notice how your body feels and when you feel tired or sleepy you should take a rest or even a short nap. You may be surprised at how good you feel after a nap and how much energy you have to take on the rest of your day.

N is for Nap

Nap Lesson

Draw yourself taking a nap. Make sure to include all the comfortable things you like (pillow, blanket, stuffed animal).

When you go home after school or after an activity, find a place where you can get comfortable and take a short nap or rest.

Be sure and tell someone how good you feel after your nap.

"I feel _____ since I took a nap."

good	hungry	rested
happy		ready to go

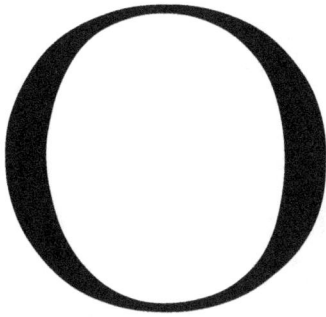

O is for **Open**—
your mind to see the
world around you.

When you open a door or a window
you can see what is on the other side. You
may need to look out the door or window for
a while before you see something you like or
see something you enjoy watching.

When you open your mind it means
you are letting yourself think that things
could get better even when it may seem
gloomy.

If something is not going the way you
want, you should think of the open door and
understand that if you keep it open other
things will come by that you want or enjoy.
But, if you keep the door closed nothing can
come in. When the door is open, be patient
and wait a little…good things will come
your way.

When you open your mind like you open the door you will see, and experience, new things.

Keeping an open mind permits you to be tolerant and accepting. A closed mind will limit your options. An open mind will provide you with many more opportunities.

O is for Open

<u>Open Lesson</u>

Can you see what is on the other side of this door?

Circle your answer or write your answer below.

Yes   or   No

_____   or   _____

If you open the door can you see what is on
the other side?

Circle your answer or write your answer
below.

Yes   or   No

_____   or   _____

Explain your answer to someone:

Why can, or can't, you see what is on the
other side?

If we open our minds like the door can we see and understand more of what is around us?

Circle your answer or write your answer below.

Yes   or   No

_____ or _____

3-Step Review—M, N, O

M is for Mindful—Be where your
feet are.

N is for Nap—take one and feel
refreshed.

O is for Open—your mind to see the
world around you.

Let's go over the last three
positive attributes we learned. M is for
Mindful. We need to pay attention to
what is going on around us and not
always look at our phones or handheld
devices.

N is for **Nap**. We should try to
take a few minutes each day to relax
and maybe even take a short nap to feel
refreshed and ready to go again.

O is for **Open**. To open your mind means that you will take the time to think about things. You will think and understand that sometimes things are different than they first appear.

Step 1

<u>Trace</u> the letters M, N, O using your finger and <u>say</u> the letter name aloud.

Step 2

Color the letter "M" **purple**,

Color the letter "N" **black**,

Color the letter "O" **brown**.

Step 3

Draw a circle.

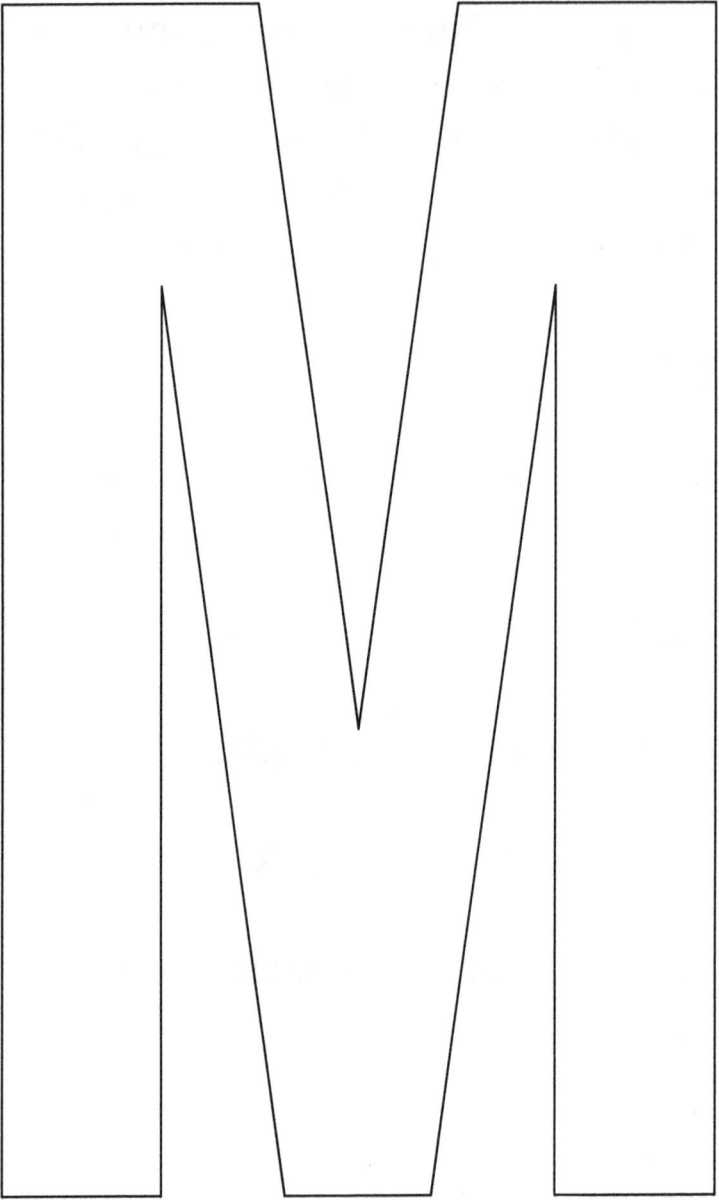

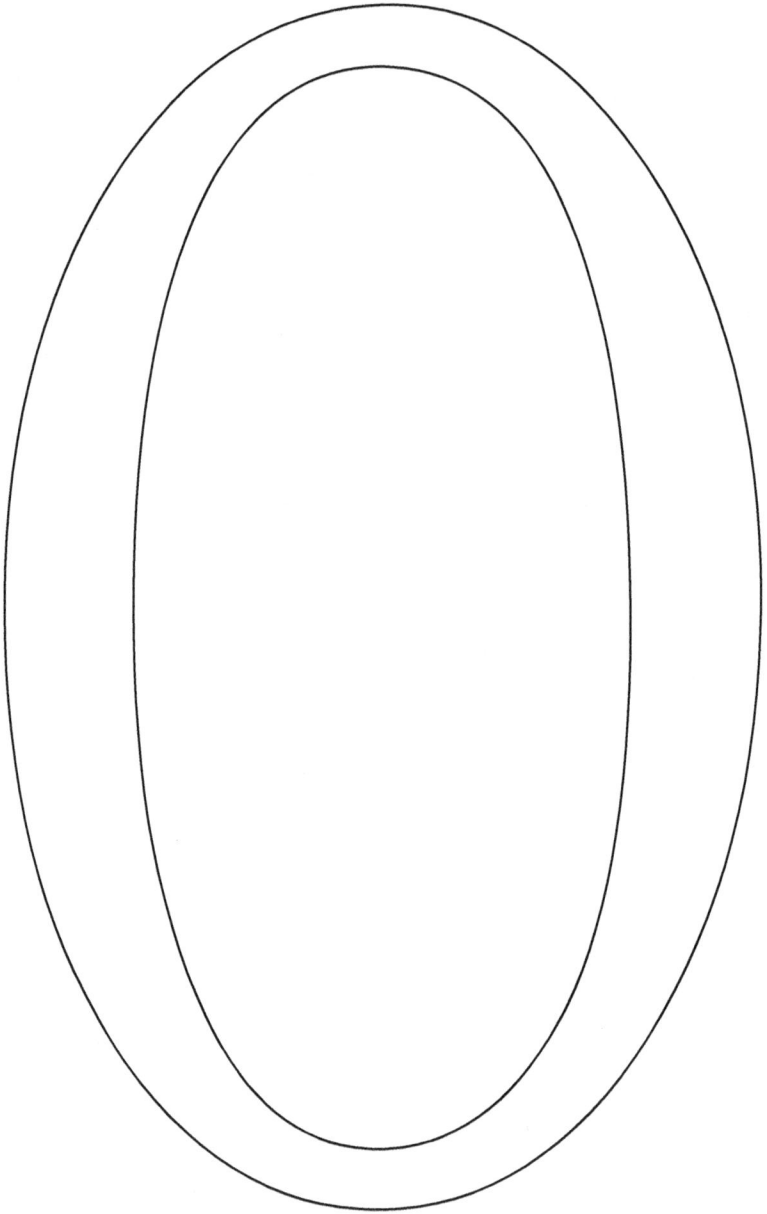

P is for **Patience**— slow down, take your time.

Do you get upset when you have to wait for something? We tend to want things right now but we have to learn to wait our turn.

When you calmly wait your turn in school at the playground or for a ride at an amusement park, you are practicing patience.

Patience is when you are able to wait on something important to you. Patience is when you take on a difficult task and you calmly set about achieving that task without complaining.

You will soon learn, when you are patient while waiting for something you are helping those around you learn patience too.

Maybe we all need to be reminded to slow down, take our time, and wait.

Patience is catchy. If you remain calm you'll see those around you will likely remain calm as well.

So when you feel yourself getting upset and complaining about the wait, remind yourself of the word patience and its meaning.

Remember, patience is catchy.

P is for Patience

Patience Lesson

From what you just read about patience, answer the following.

Patience means to _____.

Explain times when you may need to have patience.

For example, I will use patience…

"While waiting my turn at the bus stop."

I will use patience …

_____

_____

_____

I will use patience …

_____

_____

_____

Your Best
by Barbara Vance

If you always try your best
Then you'll never have to wonder
About what you could have done
If you'd summoned all your thunder.

And if your best
Was not as good
As you hoped it would be,
You still could say,
"I gave today
All that I had in me."

Q

is for **Quit**— NEVER do this.

Winston Churchill, a popular leader of Great Britain, once said, "Never, never, never quit." If you remember this simple sentence you will achieve success and learn a lot of new things along the way.

There is so much to learn as a kid. You learn the ABCs, colors and shapes. You quickly learn how to tie your shoes and ride a bike. But if you quit you would never learn any of these things.

Not quitting can make anything possible. If you quit when things get rough you won't accomplish things and you'll have nothing to look forward to.

Let's pretend you are learning to tie

your shoes. There are steps to learning how to tie your shoes. Most kids don't learn all the steps on their first try. But if you keep practicing, learning one step at a time, and not quitting, you will be so proud of yourself for learning to tie your shoes.

Sometimes you want to give up because it seems hard and you are tired of trying. That is when you take a break from trying. Taking a break is not the same as quitting. When you take a break you will be ready to try again later.

Q is for Quit

Quit Lesson

My Pledge to NOT Give up

I will not quit without trying and trying again.

I will take a break from learning and then I will try again.

_____

Write your name here

R is for **Respect**— show this in action and words.

Maybe you've heard the word respect but are still not sure what it means.

You can have respect for people, respect for things and respect for places. Respect is noticing how important someone or something is. Showing respect for someone is demonstrated in the way you talk or act with that person.

Showing respect for something is displayed by the way you take care when handling something belonging to yourself or another person.

Let's say you have your own bedroom, and in your bedroom your own toys. You would want others to respect your bedroom and toys. You wouldn't want anyone to mess up your room or break your toys, right?

When you show respect for your parents or other adults you speak nicely to them and ask for things using "please" in your question, and "thank you" in your response.

Respect is also shown in the way you act. You show respect by holding the door for another person or cleaning up after you are done playing.

Respect is an important quality—and one that will help get respect in return.

R is for Respect

Respect Lesson

Answer YES or NO to these questions about respect. Then explain your answer.

Is it respectful to hold the door open for someone and allow them to walk in front of you?

YES or NO. Explain.

Is it respectful to say "No" to your parent or grandparents when they ask you to help clear the kitchen table?

YES or NO. Explain.

Is it respectful to take care of your friend's bike that you borrowed?

YES or NO. Explain.

Can you think of a situation when you showed or used words of respect?

YES or NO. Share.

3-Step Review—P, Q, R

P is for Patience—slow down, take
your time.

Q is for Quit—NEVER do this.

R is for Respect—show this in action
and words.

    Let's go over the last three
attributes we learned. P is for
Patience. Remember to take your time
and wait your turn.

    Q is for **Quit** and you never want
to do this. Adults are always telling
you what not to do and quitting is one
of them. Don't quit. Keep trying or
look for another way to get it done.

    R is for **Respect.** Be sure to
respect your friends and family by
showing them you care and are helpful.

Remember being respectful is also being a good listener.

Step 1

Trace the letters P, Q, R using your finger and say the letter name aloud.

Step 2

Color the letter "P" **red**,

Color the letter "Q" **gray**,

Color the letter "R" **pink**.

Step 3

Draw a square.

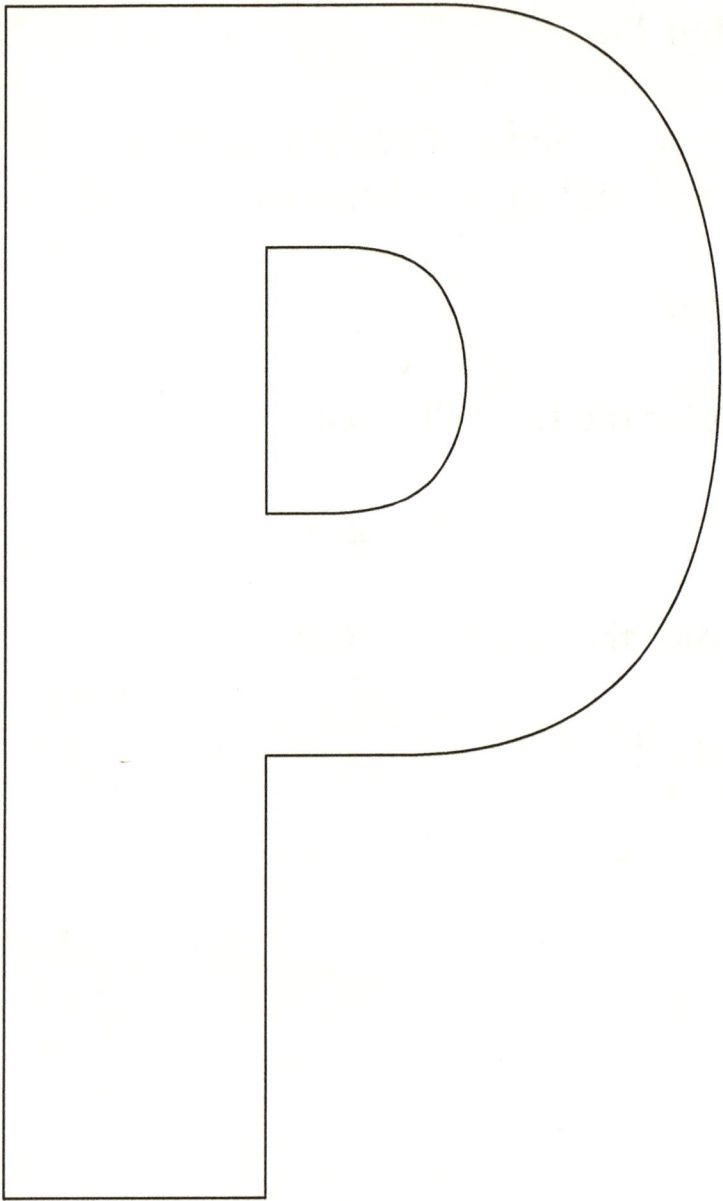

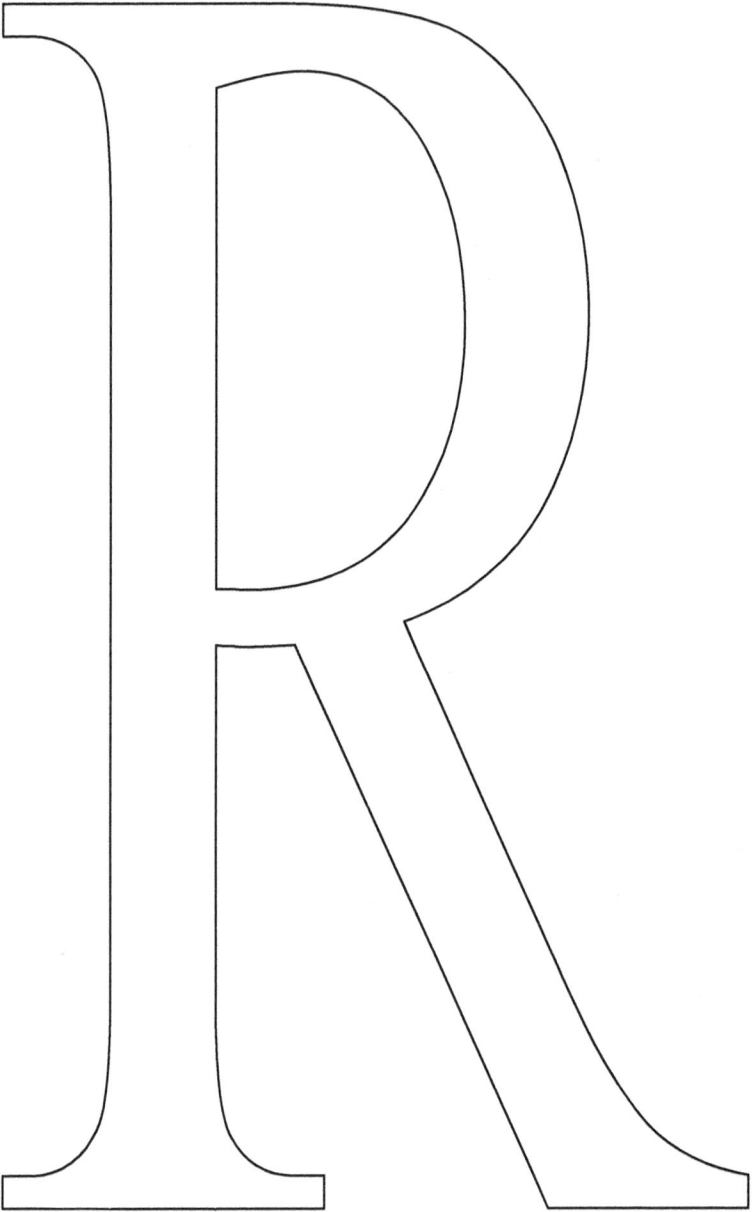

S

is for **Sibling**—
a brother or sister.

A sibling is a brother or a sister. There are different types of siblings—they all have a special bond. You may have a sibling, a half-sibling, or a step-sibling.

In all three sibling situations you have a family bond. Sometimes one of the sibling bonds is stronger than another but that is between you and your brother, sister, half-brother, half-sister, step-brother or step-sister.

We can show our love and respect to our siblings in different ways. Since we often live with our siblings and see them every day we sometimes forget to talk and show love and respect.

Efforts should be made to listen to

what our siblings have to say and to respond in a nice way. A little more kindness, understanding and love should be given to your siblings.

Family bonds are precious and to be celebrated regardless of the biological relationship.

S is for Sibling

Sibling Lesson

Draw or write a **Sibling Kindness Plan** on how to you can show love and kindness to your siblings.

Draw a picture, make a craft, or help your sibling with a project. Use the space to create your kindness plan.

My Sibling Kindness Plan.

T

is for **Task**—
do one and save-a-step.

Let's think of a large cake cut into many small slices. If we want the entire cake to be eaten we would need a lot of people to take a slice.

Our home can be looked at the same way as the large cake. If we want our home to be clean and in order then we all need to pitch in and do small tasks every day—sort of like taking that slice of cake.

Sometimes the small task can simply be done if you "save-a-step." An example of how you save-a-step is when you eat a snack you don't walk away from what you leave behind. Clean up after yourself—right away. That way you don't have to go back to clean it up later—you will save-a-step ☺.

If you get used to cleaning up after yourself and everyone in your home does the same you save time and have a neat and clean house all the time.

You could explain to your family what it means to save-a-step. You may have to remind each other from time to time by saying, "remember, save-a-step."

Of course there are other tasks you can do as a family member and sometimes they may be more than pick up after yourself— you may be asked by an adult to help with a particular task.

It is also important to pay close attention and follow directions when working on a new task.

T is for Task

Task Lesson

Below are some tasks, or chores, you could offer to do at home. These chores are listed by age.

If you are 3-5 years old you can:

O Put dirty clothes in the hamper

O Make your bed

O Dust baseboard

O Take out recycling

O Match socks

O Fold dish towels

O Feed pets

If you are 6-8 years old you can do all of the above plus:

O Help prepare a meal

O Fold or hang laundry

O Get mail

O Rake leaves

U

is for **Universal**—
learn this language.

A lot of gestures that we use are understood by people who live in other countries.

A lot of gestures that people of other countries use, we understand as well.

Some of the obvious gestures are a wave of your hand to mean "hello," a smile as a way to greet someone, or a handshake to welcome someone.

These are called universal gestures and are understood by many cultures.

From an early age we are taught a universal language before we learn to speak. A thumbs up means "okay." A "high five" is a way to celebrate or cheer.

A movement with your hand to initiate the drinking of a glass of water may tell someone you are thirsty.

When you meet someone who doesn't speak your language, don't hesitate to speak the universal language and SMILE.

U is for Universal

Universal Lesson

See if you can name what each gesture might mean.

_____

_____

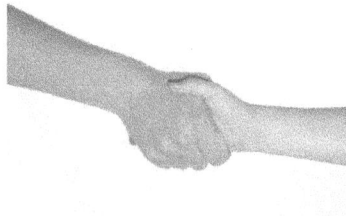

_____

3-Step Review—S, T, U

S is for Sibling—a brother or sister.

T is for Task—do one and save-a-step.

U is for Universal—learn this language.

Let's go over the last three positive attributes we learned. S is for **Sibling**. There are three types of siblings—half-sibling, step-sibling, or a full biological sibling.

T is for **Task**. Doing a small task can save-a-step for the next person. Continue to do your share of the household tasks.

U is for **Universal**. There are some gestures that mean the same in many countries. This universal language includes communicating through a friendly wave, smile or handshake.

Step 1

Trace the letters S, T, U using your finger and say the letter name aloud.

Step 2

Color the letter "S" **yellow,**

Color the letter "T" **orange,**

Color the letter "U" **blue.**

Step 3

Draw whatever shape you like.

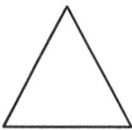

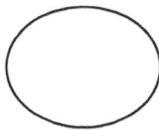

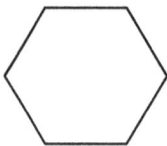

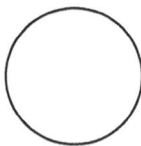

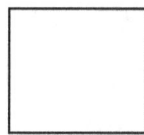

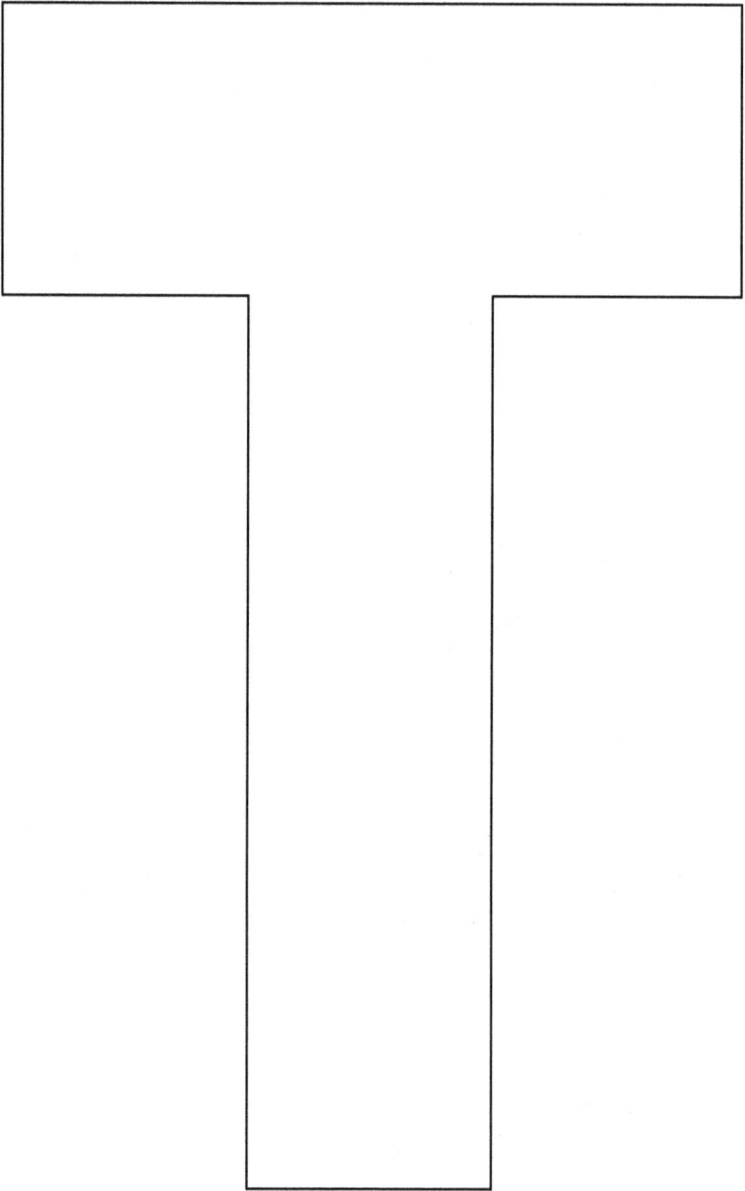

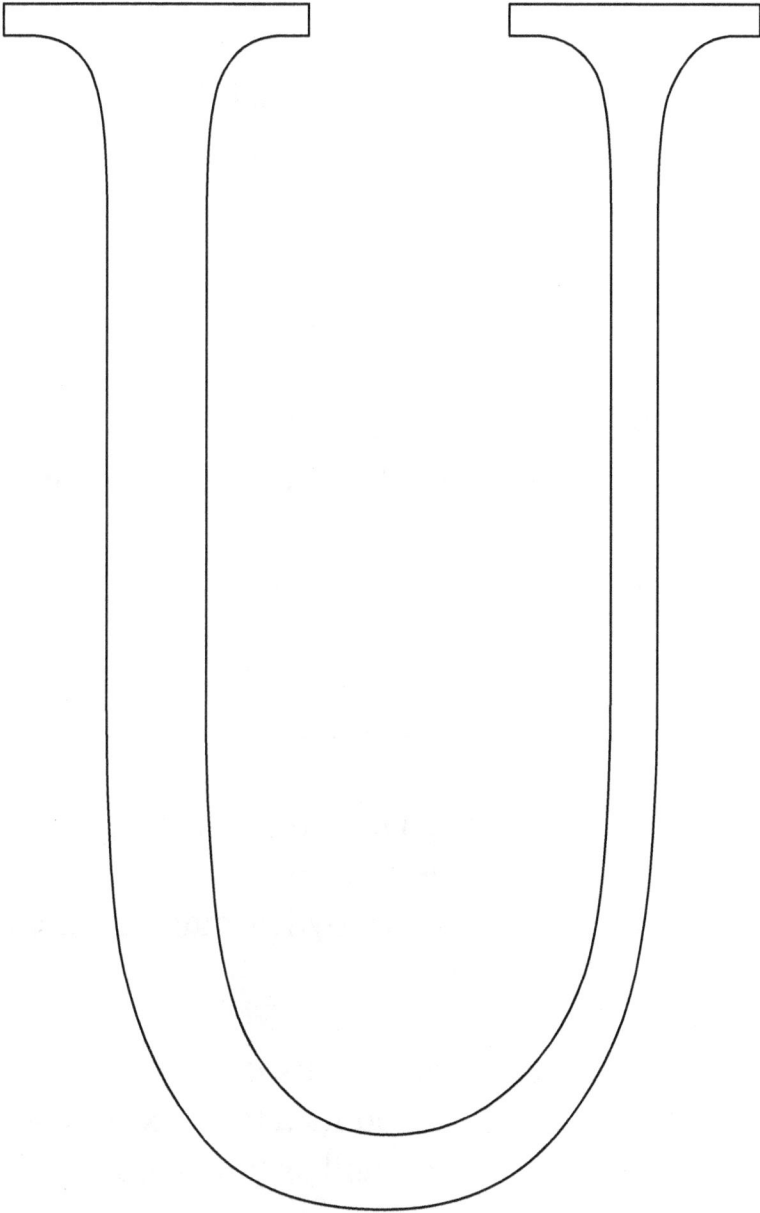

V

is for **Victory**—when you reach your goals.

Winning is exciting. We want to win when we play a game or compete in a sport.

What can be even more exciting is when we have an idea of what we want to learn or do—this is called a goal—then we set out to reach that goal.

Maybe your goal is to learn to tie your shoes, ride a bicycle or dribble a basketball. Once you reach victory by learning that goal you should set a new goal.

Thinking of new goals is not just for kids. It is a really good idea to work on your goals as you grow up and as you get older.

Your goals will change but the good feeling you get when you reach it will always feel the same. It is a victory.

V is for Victory

Victory Lesson

It is time for you to think of **2** goals for yourself so that you can feel the victory.

Examples—

I will learn to tie my shoes by next month.

OR

I will complete one chore around the house every day.

You can draw, write or tell someone your 2 goals:

#1 goal:

#2 goal:

W

is for **Whisper—** the softest of your soft voice.

Have you ever been told "Shhh, keep your voice down," or "Please use your inside voice?"

We have two voices—one is soft and one is loud. As you grow older you learn more about when to use your soft voice and when it is okay to use your loud voice. You learn by listening to how others are using their voice. Are they talking with a soft voice or a loud voice?

Before going someplace, ask your parent what kind of voice you should use— soft or loud.

A whisper is the softest voice and you might whisper while in church. To cheer or yell is your loudest voice and you would cheer at a football game or outside while playing with friends.

W is for Whisper

Whisper Lesson

Let's practice when to use your soft voice and when to use your loud voice.

Listed below are a few examples of places you may visit once in a while. If you think you should use your *soft* voice write an "S" on the line. If you think you could use your **LOUD** voice, write an "L" on the line.

_____ An airplane full of people.

_____ A restaurant.

_____ A soccer game.

_____ Baby napping in the house.

_____ Playing outside with friends.

I'm Glad to be Me
by XCBVIA

I'm glad to be me,
I'm glad to be who I am,
I'd rather be,
no one but myself,

because I am unique,
I am special,
I am a one of a kind,
made by my LORD above,

I do things different than everybody else,
I don't try to be someone I'm not,
I AM ME,
and I'M GLAD,
SO GLAD,
I'm glad to be unique,
I'm glad to be me.

X

is for **eXample**—
set a good one.

You can be a leader by setting a good example for others. Children who are younger than you will watch how you talk to people, how you treat others and how you treat them—so set a good example.

One way to set a good example is when you include other children in a game that you and your friends are playing. Another good example is when you help Grandma carry her groceries into the house or help a classmate understand the lesson in class that they are having trouble with.

Whatever it is that you do with others or for others, try to always be the person that sets a good example. Understand that there are always people around that will see the good that you are doing. And maybe, other young children will follow your example and be leaders too by setting a good example.

X is for eXample

eXample Lesson

For each of the following situations, tell someone what you could do that would be a good example for others.

1. You are shopping with your parents and ask them to buy you a toy. They tell you they are sorry but they can't buy the toy for you today.

   a. How can you respond so that you set a good example for others?

   b. What might not be a good way to respond?

2. A boy, younger than you, is on the playground sitting alone and crying.

   a. How can you respond so you set a good example for others?

   b. What might not be a good way to respond?

3-Step Review—V, W, X

V is for Victory—when you reach your goals.

W is for Whisper—for the softest of your soft voice.

X is for eXample—set a good one.

Let's go over the last three positive attributes. V is for **Victory** and this focuses on reaching goals to improve yourself.

W is for **Whisper** reminding you to be aware of where you are and to speak only as loud as is appropriate.

X is for **eXample**. It is important for all of us to set good examples of behavior.

Step 1

Trace the letters V, W, X using your finger and say the letter name aloud.

Step 2

Color the letter "V" **purple**,

Color the letter "W" **green**,

Color the letter "X" **black**.

Step 3

Draw whatever shape you like.

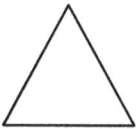

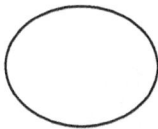

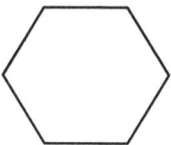

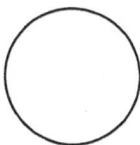

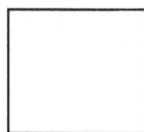

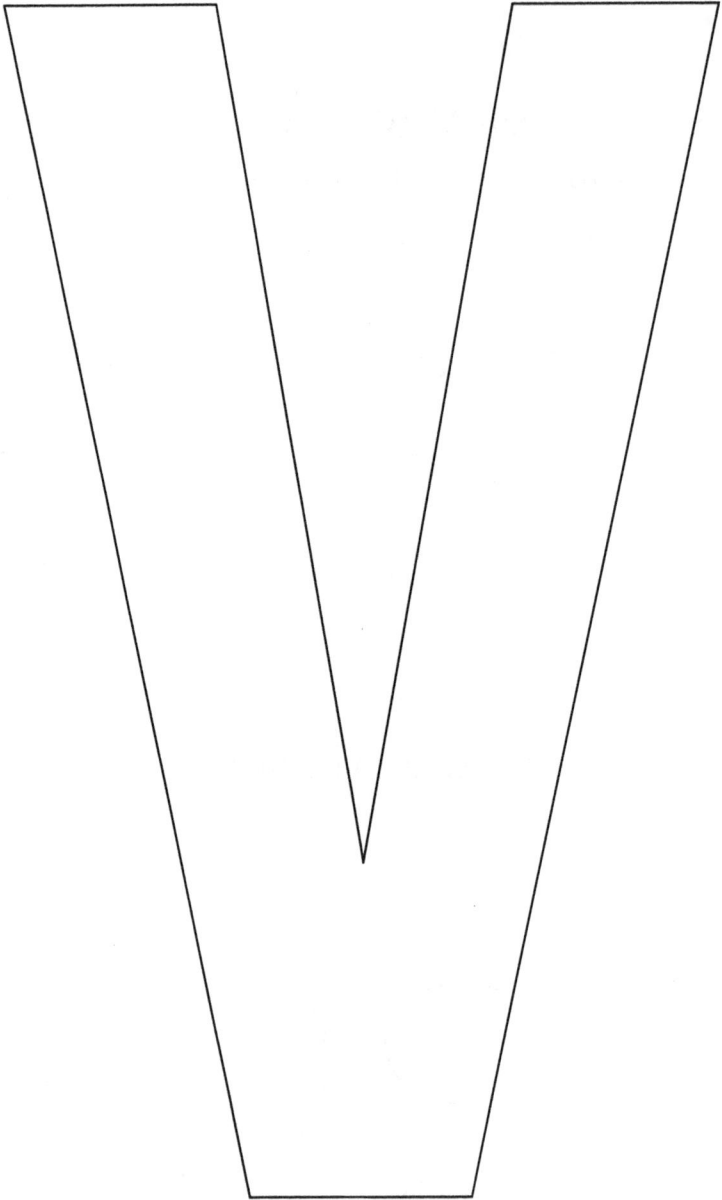

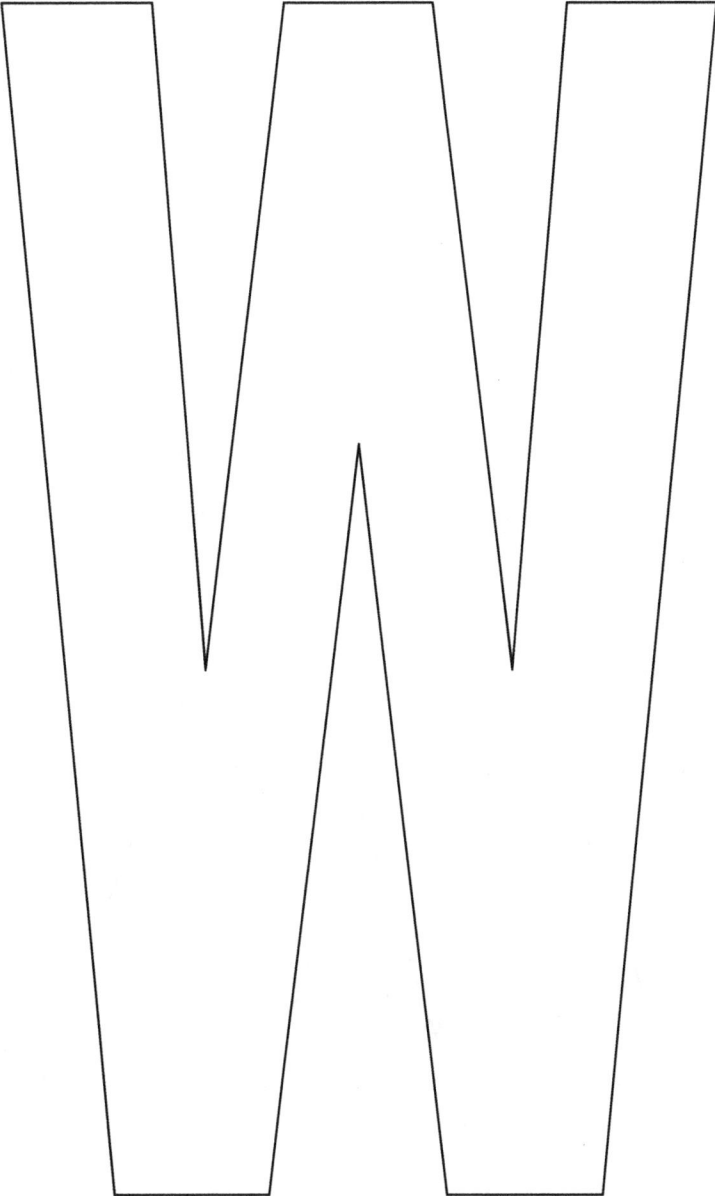

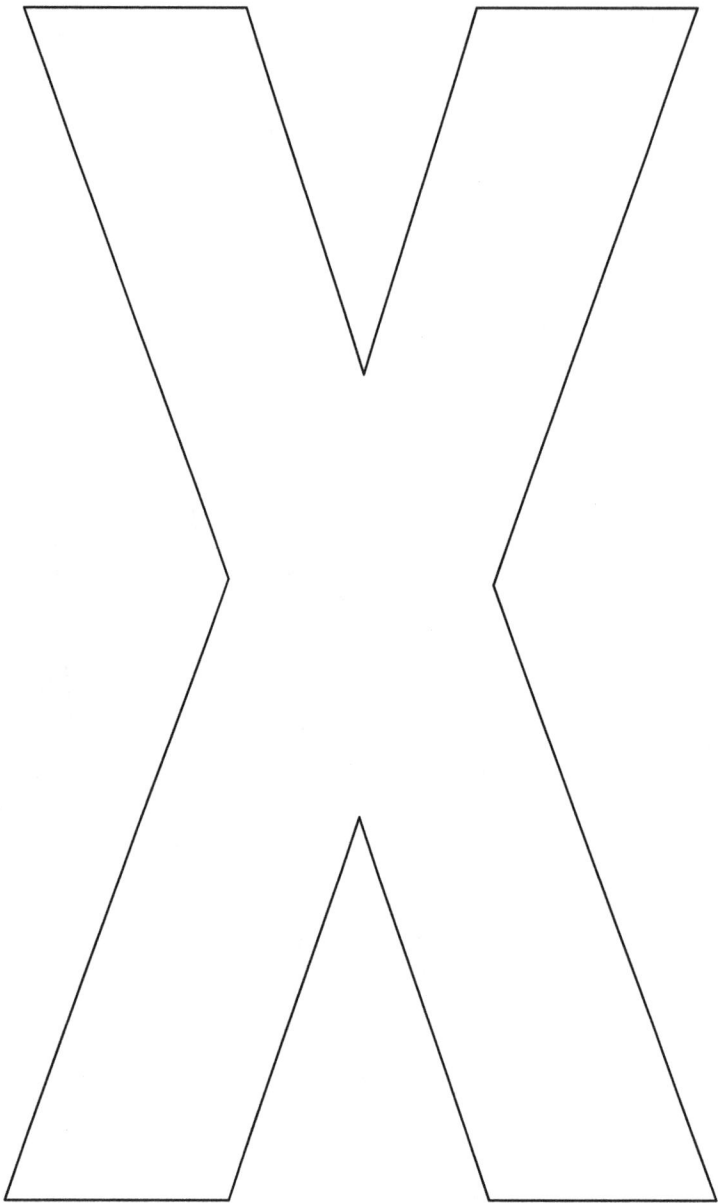

Y

is for **Yearn**—
to learn more &
more (& more).

To yearn for something is to want it badly—you might dream about what it is you want or you might wish for something with all your heart.

Perhaps you dream about learning to swim, which means you yearn to swim. You think about swimming and desire to swim.

Yearning to learn is good because it means you keep moving forward, looking towards the next accomplishment and new learning. Yearning to learn may be what you need to set new goals.

Share with someone what you yearn for right now. The word yearn may be a new word for some people but they will be glad to hear you talk about what you yearn to learn.

Learning new things is a way to fuel your body with information. Continue to work to keep your desire to learn alive.

Y is for Yearn

Lesson for Yearn

How will you keep your yearn for learning strong? Practice with these ideas.

1. Set your mind to learn something new about something that you are interested in. For example, if you are interested in giraffes, learn some new information about giraffes. Yearn to learn new information—to *want* to know more.

2. Yearn and get excited for the next chance you have to learn something new.

Z

is for **Zebra**—
what color are your
stripes?

We are all very different people who learn, play, work, and grow together.

Often times we might look and act like members of the same family but even in our own family we have different "stripes" or interests.

When you describe yourself and the things you like, the things you don't like, what you are good at and what you find hard to do, you are defining your stripes. Just like a zebra, we all have different stripes— different strengths and weaknesses.

You and your sibling might both like pizza and playing baseball but more than likely you each dislike something the other likes. That is okay. It is okay to have different stripes. In fact, it would be way too boring if we all had the same stripes and liked and disliked the exact same things.

By having different stripes, we are making life interesting and full of color. Those with different stripes can teach us about their interests and we can teach them about our stripes—our interests.

Welcome those that are different than you—you just might find out how interesting life can be.

Z is for Zebra

Lesson for Zebra

Your challenge is to learn more about your friends. See what kind of stripes they have and share your stripes too.

Ask a few of your friends some of these questions:

1. What do you like to do when you are bored?

2. Would you rather watch TV or play outside?

3. Do you like to eat at restaurants? If so, what is your favorite place to eat?

3-Step Review—Y, Z

Y is for Yearn—to learn more & more (&
        more).

Z is for Zebra—what color are your
        stripes?

Let's go over the final two positive attributes. Y is for **Yearn** and this means to always WANT to learn more. There is always more for us to learn.

Z is for **Zebra** and this reminds us that we all have different interests, like zebras all have different stripes—but this is also what makes life interesting.

Step 1

Trace the letters Y, Z using your finger and say the letter name aloud.

Step 2

Color the letter "Y" **brown,**

Color the letter "Z" **gray.**

Step 3

Draw whatever shape you like.

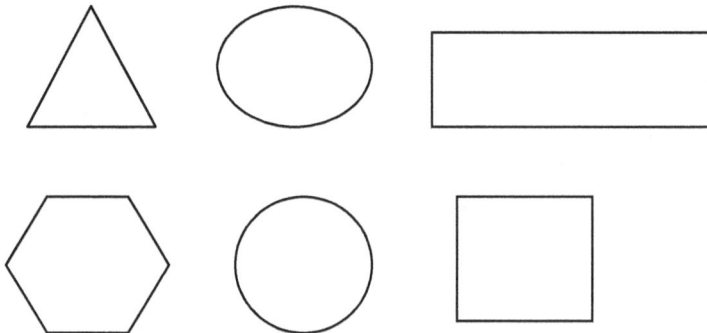

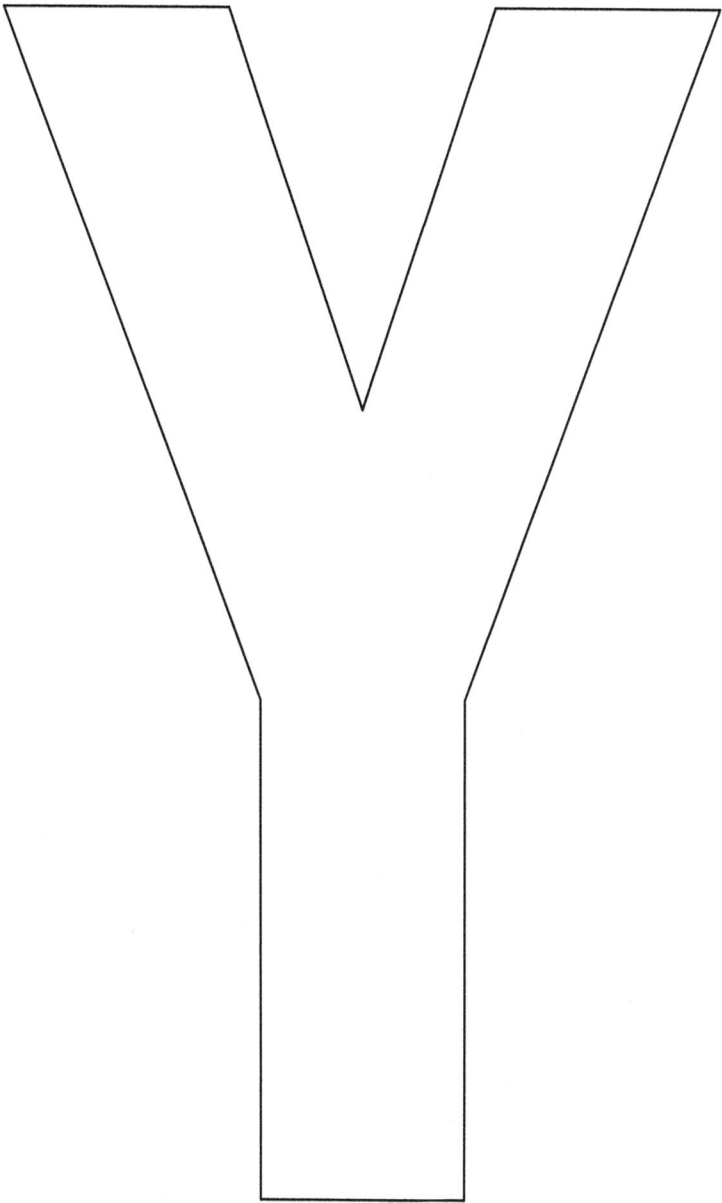

139

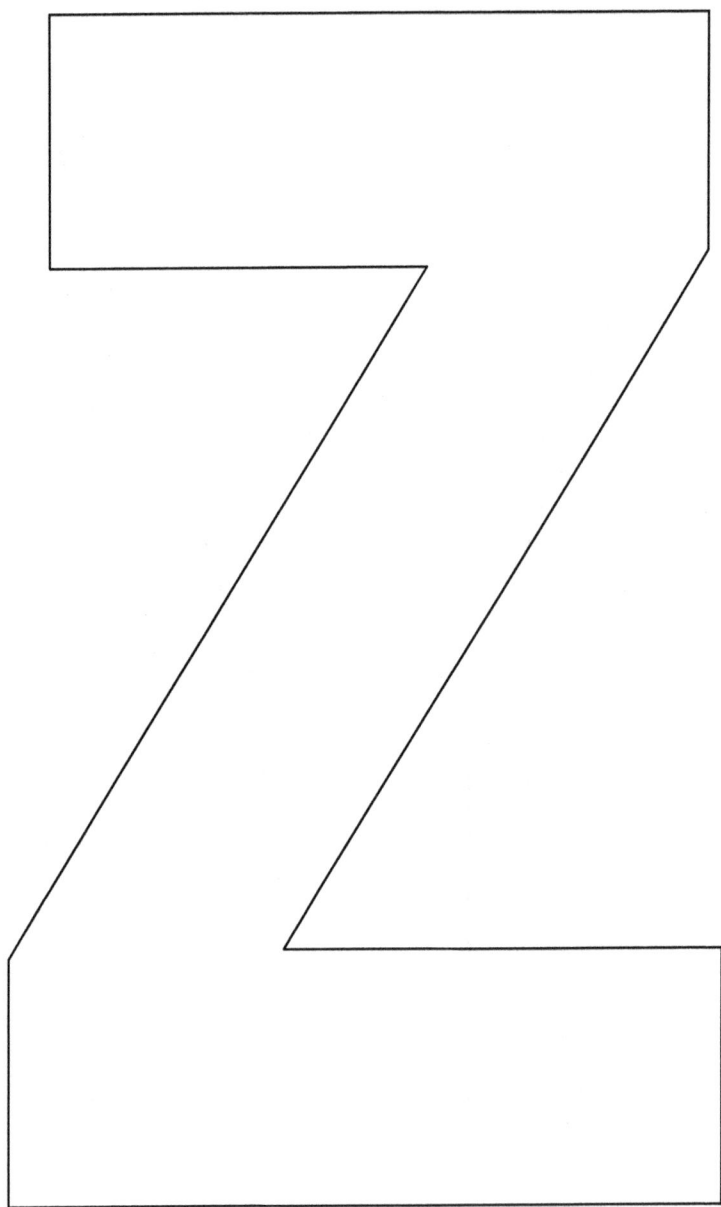

Index

About the Author

Juliann Galmarini Mangino, Ed.D. has served as a counselor and life coach for teen parents for nearly 20 years. While working full-time as a life coach, Juliann received her doctorate degree from the University of Pittsburgh. Her doctoral dissertation, *Voices of Teen Mothers: Their Challenges, Support Systems and Successes,* explored the skills and character traits that helped keep teen parents in high school and achieve graduation.

ABCs for Me! A workbook for the young learner and *ABCs for Me! Interactive strategies for the new learner, Pre-K to K* are the third and fourth book in the *Young Parenting Series*. Juliann's hope is to begin the development of positive character traits early when a child forms habits that can last a lifetime.

The newly designed *ABCs for Me! Interactive strategies for the new learner, Pre-K to K* book has larger font, fun artwork and an easy-to-follow format for the younger student.

Following the format in the *ABCs for Me!* workbook, the interactive strategies is a larger size student book which includes only the Power Lessons and review sections that follow each introduced positive character trait—allowing more room for small hands to write big.

Juliann's books, *ABCs for Mommy!* and *ABCs for Daddy!,* have been enthusiastically received and have sold thousands of copies nationwide.

Additionally, Juliann's *ABCs for Me!* books are listed by the Pennsylvania Office of Child Development and Early Learning as a suggested Social and Emotional curriculum.

Juliann earned her Masters in Counseling Education K-12 from Westminster College in New Wilmington, Pennsylvania and Bachelor of Arts in Education from Slippery Rock University in Slippery Rock, Pennsylvania.

Every day Juliann works hard to practice what she preaches. She, along with her husband Matthew, enthusiastically—and sometimes successfully—attempt to model positive character traits for their young adult twins, Mark and Melina.

Follow Juliann's blog of positive attributes and thoughts at abcbookseries.wordpress.com or on Twitter @JuliannMangino.

www.ingramcontent.com/pod-product-compliance
Lightning Source LLC
Chambersburg PA
CBHW022025090426
42739CB00006BA/289